Dogs in Snow

Dogs in Snow

The Ultimate Collection

BLACK & WHITE PUBLISHING

First published 2015
by Black & White Publishing Ltd
29 Ocean Drive, Edinburgh EH6 6JL

1 3 5 7 9 10 8 6 4 2   15 16 17 18

ISBN: 978 1 78530 000 4

Text © Black & White Publishing 2015

A CIP catalogue record for this book is available from the British Library.

Typeset by Creative Link, North Berwick

Printed and bound by IMAGO

Images used on p2, p4, p5, p10, p13, p17, p19, p22, p24, p25, p28, p30, p31, p32, p36, p42, p43, p44, p45, p46, p48, p49, p50, p52, p53, p56, p63, p65, p66, p67, p74, p76, p77, p78, p80, p81, p82, p84, p85, p86, p88, p89, p90, p93, p94, p96, p101, p102, p104, p105, p108, p109, p110, p111, p112, p114, p115, p118, p119, p120, p124, p126, p129, p134 and p138 © Shutterstock

Images used on p6, p7, p8, p9, p12, p14, p16, p18, p20, p26, p27, p34, p35, p37, p38, p40, p41, p54, p55, p58, p59, p60, p62, p64, p68, p70, p71, p72, p73, p87, p92, p95, p98, p99, p100, p106, p114, p116, p122, p123, p128, p130, p132, p133, p136, p137 and p140 © iStock

Introduction

Dogs love snow. There's that first moment they see it and wonder what it is — and then there's no stopping them as they discover just how much fun it can be.

Some like to roll in it, some like to dig, others love snowballs and some just like running around until they fall asleep in the cold, wrapped up in their thick winter coat. *Dogs in Snow* has beautiful images of lots of different breeds doing what they do best — having fun!

From Malamutes and Huskies who are born to enjoy snowy conditions to more unlikely snow-lovers such as Yorkshire Terriers and Pugs, this uplifting collection explores the simple yet endlessly entertaining endeavours of dogs in snow. Enjoy them all as they play and frolic in the snow in this celebration of man's best friend, which shows why we love our furry companions so much. They may be outside in the snow, but these wintry dogs will truly warm your heart.

French Mastiff

Also known as the Dogue de Bordeaux, this pup is loyal and keen to please his owners — when he's not preoccupied with snowballs. He will grow to a massive size, but is loving and docile by nature.

Apricot Cockapoo

This sociable little chap is full of enthusiasm, and loves nothing more than the company of other dogs or humans. Happy-go-lucky by nature, he is happy to run around all day in the snow. Or the sunshine. Or the rain.

Border Collie

He's a dog with unlimited energy, stamina and working drive. A premier herding dog, highly trainable and intelligent. A sportsman, an athlete: agile, and obedient. Whatever the weather.

German Shepherds

They don't always get on with other members of the same breed, but these two friends put aside their differences on a snowy hillside as they demonstrate their strength, agility and appetite for fun.

Dachshund

This wirehaired puppy is not ideally suited to the snow
– with his short legs and long body he can get cold very
quickly. But he's a plucky little dog and stubborn to a fault,
so he doesn't realise how small he really is. Full of self-
assuredness, he loves to burrow, bark and chase.

Yorkshire Terrier

He loves attention and is full of self-importance, liking everything to be just a certain way. Active for his size, he enjoys a walk in the snow — but he'll let you know as soon as he's ready to come home, as he loves to bark.

Wheaten Terrier

With so much fur, this dog loves the cold — he's very energetic and in hot weather he can sometimes overheat. More laid back than other terriers, he's a friendly fellow and is known for welcoming dogs and humans alike with a slobbery 'Wheaten Greeting'.

Boerboel

Bred as a working guard-dog, this Boerboel is a big guy. But that doesn't stop him frolicking in the snow, as he is energetic and playful. Originally from South Africa, he is intelligent and devoted to his family, but needs a dominant owner.

Australian Labradoodle

Ever the enthusiast, he is always the first to dive right in. Whether it's meeting new people, frolicking in the snow or going for a swim, this plucky dog is always up for it. Relentlessly upbeat, he is a friend for everyone.

Bernese Mountain Dogs

These puppies love to be outdoors, and will grow up to be very fast runners. They need lots of exercise and were traditionally bred for farm work, but, docile and affectionate, they love to come indoors for some company after a day in the snow.

English Setter

Indoors he is a couch potato, but outdoors he is an adventurer. This friendly dog can often have a mind of his own when it comes to outdoor life, but he is a gentle soul who loves both a cuddle and a snowy expedition in equal measure.

Golden Retriever

Known for his playful and active nature, this Retriever is cooling down with a much-needed rest in the snow. Vivacious, enthusiastic and trusting, he's happy in all weathers.

Dogue de Bordeaux

Calm and loyal, this enormous dog isn't as scary as he looks. Whilst he makes a fearless guard-dog, he is also very sociable and playful, making a great companion for loving families.

Labrador

Known for her fondness of ball games, she is an expert at catching and fetching. Even if the ball is made of snow, she never misses a beat. Bouncy and vivacious, this energetic dog will keep you on your toes until she's ready for a nap.

Jack Russell

He may look like snow wouldn't melt in his mouth, but this tiny terrier is larger than life. There's a big personality behind his cute demeanour; he's stubborn, individual, intelligent and fearless.

St Bernards

These lolloping giants are slow but sturdy. Snow lovers, they don't cope well in hot weather, and too much vigorous activity can actually do them damage due to their size. Still playful and entertaining dogs, they are placid and easy to live with – although they might not all fit under the same roof.

Staffordshire Bull Terrier and Short-Haired German Shepherd

These two dogs make great running companions, as both are powerful, energetic and agile. With their endurance, these pals will keep each other entertained in the snow for hours — although the white Shepherd might have the advantage at hide-and-seek.

Maltese

Companionable, upbeat and playful, this little dog is never happier than when she's by your side wherever you go. But be careful to keep an eye on her — with little legs and a white coat she is easy to lose in the snow!

Irish Wolfhounds

Originally bred for hunting and guarding, these two belong to the tallest dog breed and are an imposing sight. A hardy ancient breed, they are happy to be outside in the snow. That said, their easy-going temperament means they are happy to be most places.

Staffordshire Bull Terriers

Despite their reputation as aggressive dogs, these girls are very sociable animals and love to play ball games — or snowball games in this case. Powerful, fearsome and loyal, this trio has both big teeth and big hearts.

Cocker Spaniel

Originally a gundog, this Spaniel loves to forage through the snow for interesting finds. A clever, energetic dog, he's as happy at home by the fire as he is rummaging through the snow.

Golden Retriever

With a water-repellent coat, the snow doesn't bother this dog. He seems more upset at finding himself alone, as he loves the company of dogs and humans alike. Confident, intelligent and fun loving, he is just waiting for someone to join in with him.

Australian Shepherd

With supreme obedience and trainability, this intelligent dog is eager to please and relishes a job to do. Originating on Western American ranches, he is as happy herding cows as he is playing Frisbee – he's just waiting for his next command.

Lhasa Apso

Clumps of ice can't slow this stubborn dog down. Devoted to his owner and a superb guard dog, this little guy has a will — and a hairstyle — all of his own.

Jack Russell

Lively, independent and clever, this short-haired little dog is charming and affectionate, but is also a mischievous little scamp. He'll always find the loophole in any command you give, and loves to chew, dig and bark. The quickest way to spot him in snow is to look for the nearest flurry shooting into the air.

Miniature American Eskimo Dog

Bubbly and outgoing, this striking dog has a personality the size of his wardrobe. He is highly biddable and tries hard to please his owner, fitting into family life perfectly. Descended from the German Spitz, he loves the cold weather and wears his jumper purely for decoration as his fluffy coat keeps him warm enough.

Dalmatian

With his trademark black spots, he can always be spotted in the snow. He's got strength and stamina, so he loves running and hiking and hates to be without a job. If he is in need of one, he'll occupy himself by digging huge craters until your garden looks as spotty as he does.

Pug

Strutting his stuff, this puppy is ready to strike a pose no matter what the time of year. Famous for his sassy attitude, he has a lot of confidence for such a small dog. He loves to sleep and can snore the house down, but when he's awake he is vivacious, attentive and will do anything to get your attention. He's a celebrity in the making.

Corgi-Jack Russell

Waiting for his next command, he's an obedient dog who knows there's a ball chase through the snow if he's well behaved.

Golden Retriever and Springer Spaniel

Never likely to pass up an opportunity to mess around, this lively duo will give each other a run for their money: they're both agile, bouncy and have bundles of energy. Sociable and gentle, they love the company of other dogs. Chances are the snow will have melted before they've stopped playing.

Springer Spaniel

Living up to his name, this Springer prefers to leap and bounce over the snow rather than walk through it. Brimming with energy, he is alert, attentive and athletic. When you can catch him sitting still he loves a cuddle, but it won't be long before he's off again.

West Highland Terrier

Clever and cheeky, it won't be long before this innocent-looking dog is causing mischief. He loves to chase and roughhouse, but it's all in good fun as he's friends with everybody and is too chirpy to take seriously.

Siberian Husky

Taking a rare moment of down-time, this happy Husky is waiting to start work pulling the sledge

Havanese

This little toy dog is surprisingly sturdy. She is spirited and lively, but once she's up to her nose in snow she often realises that she's not quite so suited to the outdoors. Still happy to give anything a go, she'll dive right in if she thinks it will make her owners happy.

Fox Terrier

A fearless explorer, the snow is no match for this wiry-haired fellow. Come to think of it, not much is! A spirited dog, he can be wilful and adventurous outdoors without supervision, but it's not his fault - all he really needs is a playmate who can keep up with him.

crossbreed

Nothing can stand between this dog and his goal — not even two feet of snow.

Crossbreed

Is it a bird? Is it a plane? This little scruffy superhero won't be slowed down by the snow — he's on a mission!

Border Collie

Taking a moment of well earned downtime, this obedient dog is one for all weathers. Happiest when he's active, he is ready to get back to working or playing just as soon as you are.

Siberian Husky

He's a well-known escape artist once he's older, happy to dig his way under a fence if you're not careful. Athletic and intelligent, he can be independent and challenging. With a thick coat, he's bred for the depths of Siberia and only feels at home in the deepest, coldest snow.

Jack Russell

Doing what he does best, this tiny dog is showing off his large bark to the snowy surroundings. Whether he's happy, sad or angry, he'll be sure to tell you, as he likes his opinions to be heard.

Airedale Terriers

Rough and tough, this duo is intelligent and versatile. Good hunters, they are fearless and protective, but they also have a playful and loving nature. They're easily distracted by their more base instincts and don't always listen to orders when they have their noses in the snow.

West Highland Terrier

An alert and spirited dog, he always has an eye on the horizon for something small to chase. He's robust, with a thick undercoat and self-assured nature, so he's happy to roam the snowy landscape by himself — but he's always pleased to meet a few friends to socialise with along the way.

Siberian Husky

An impressive sled dog used to life in extreme conditions, he would work, eat and sleep in the snow if necessary.

Golden Retriever

Overjoyed at the arrival of the snow, he's always looking for another reason to be cheerful.

Alaskan Malamute

With a powerful body built for stamina and strength, this intelligent dog needs a job to stop him becoming bored. At his best in the snow, he loves pulling heavy sleds over long distances, or even just having a rest from time to time.

Golden Retrievers

Gentle by nature, these dogs still love to roughhouse when they play. Although they're not dominant and are always happy to share, this friendly pair decided it was fairest to have a ball each. Bred to retrieve, they will play a game of fetch for hours without getting cold feet.

Bichon Frise

A merry dog, she is an attention seeker and needs human company to thrive. Sensitive and affectionate, she is the ultimate companion and will do anything to be by your side.

Golden Retriever

He's loving and obedient, but he can also be a bit of a clown at times. The snow brings out his playful side, but he'll beg you to join in the games with him as he's happiest when he's by your side.

Miniature Poodles and Doodles

A sociable bunch, they love the company of other dogs and people. Playful and intelligent, they need constant physical and mental stimulation. However, they are easily trainable and eager to please, so getting them to pose for a photo isn't too difficult.

Border Collie

On icy ground it's even harder to get this energetic dog to grind to a halt.

Cairn Terrier

He's curious, animated, tough, and he's been doing his favourite thing: digging. More likely to be found burrowing into the snow than running around in it, he's a strong-minded and entertaining character who loves the outdoors.

Samoyed

This fluffy dog is so used to the snow that it's hard to tell where the snow ends and the dog begins. Bred in Siberia, she is an expert reindeer herder and sledge-puller. When she's at home, however, she's a loving, playful and gentle companion, known for her characteristic smile.

Chow Chow

An ancient breed from northern China, the Chow Chow — or 'fluffy lion dog' — is now popular worldwide for its unique appearance. He is a protective and fearless dog, and rarely even notices when it snows.

West Siberian Laika

Originating in Russia, this wolf-like dog is no stranger to the cold. Whilst he is an expert hunter by nature, he is more interested in rolling around in the snow this time. He is intensely loyal and loves being out and about with his owner in any weather.

Labrador

Almost as white as the snow, this cheeky chappy is fun-loving, affectionate and devoted. Intelligent, focused and incredibly observant, this pup could grow up to be anything from a guide dog to a lifeguard.

Cocker Spaniel

In classic Cocker style, this red spaniel might have been a little too eager to play in the snow and dived right in at the deep end.

Old English Sheepdog

Originally bred to herd sheep, despite looking quite a lot like one himself, his fluffy coat keeps him warm in all weathers. He can be strong-willed, but loves being part of a family.

Lagotto Romagnolo

She loves to dig, and judging by her snowy snout she's been doing just that. A pensive dog, she is unsatisfied without a job to do and is always sniffing or listening for anything out of the ordinary. Easily bored without a challenge, you'll have to work hard to keep her on her toes.

Beagle

Being a scent hound, this dog has an extremely sensitive nose – let's hope the same can't be said for the snowman. He's gentle and playful, but his natural instincts can make him scatty and distractible. If he picks up a scent he will often chase it, making him a great tracker dog.

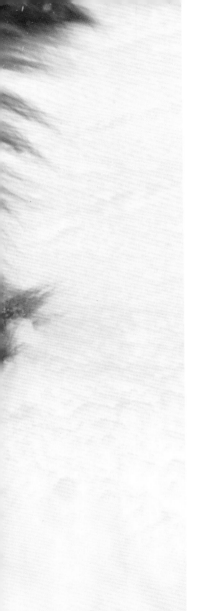

Husky-Chow Chow Mix

This peculiar crossbreed — the 'Chusky' — is a playful and affectionate dog with a laid-back attitude. His gorgeous red colour stands out against the snow, but he's looking forward to a sleep and a stroke once he's done showing off.

German Shepherd

They might be little, but these puppies won't let that stop them enjoying the snow. Wilful and independent, they have all the makings of a true German Shepherd.

English Cocker Spaniel

He's a vibrant and happy dog, always keen to please everyone around him. But in between people-pleasing, he can't resist the urge to let his hair down and play in the snow.

Golden Retrievers

Making the most of the snow while the grown-ups are away, these pups are happy just playing amongst themselves. Intelligent and lively, they know how to turn the snow from a blank canvas into a puppy playground.

Great Dane

This gentle giant doesn't know his own size, and really thinks he's a lapdog. He craves human affection and will take up most of the sofa just to be next to you. He loves to gambol along with you in the snow, but his favourite place is at home by the fire.

Alaskan Malamute

Whilst frolicking in the snow has been enough to tire out this pup, it will take a lot more to wear him out when he grows up, as he has been bred to pull heavy cargo through the snow. Used to harsh conditions, he is independent and instinctive, but he loves to please his owner just as much as he loves to run and hunt.

Miniature Schnauzer

Alert and friendly, this playful dog is far from the 'grumpy old man' to which he is so often referred. Whilst his beard and eyebrows can give him a serious air, he's an energetic and fun-loving dog — more of a Santa Claus than a Scrooge!

West Highland Terrier

He's only got little legs, so the snow can pose a challenge. More likely to plough his way through the snow than walk through it, he doesn't let it bother him. A big dog in a little dog's body, he's so full of self-esteem that he knows he's the best thing around. He's friendly and happy, with a lively nature that endears him to everyone.

Weimaraner

Sunshine or snow, day or night, this dog has one speed: running. Full of energy, he needs constant activity to keep him entertained. Loyal and athletic, he is the ultimate outdoor dog, epitomising speed, stamina, and agility.

St Bernard

Accustomed to his snowy surroundings, this gentle dog is bred for mountain rescue. He may not look too cheerful, but he is characteristically docile, content and eminently loveable – despite his tendency to drool.

Golden Retriever

A playful pup who's eager to learn, he has a passion for the great outdoors. He's keen to please and once he's learned the ropes he'll be the most reliable pet you've ever had.

Tibetan Terrier

Traditionally good luck charms for Tibetan monks, this ancient dog is friendly and feisty. Aware of his cultural importance, this assertive canine knows what he likes and what he doesn't like. With a resistant coat and flat, snowshoe feet, he definitely likes the snow.

Golden Retriever

Whilst he might look a little sad, this gentle dog loves the outdoors and is known for being cheerful and playful all year round. A canine of many talents, he is a fantastic gun dog by breed. But his intelligent and caring nature also qualifies him as a great guide dog candidate or a loveable, popular family pet.

Jack Russell

Full of personality, he might not be of much use in the snow but he is certainly great company. Resolute and energetic, he is determined to make the most of any outing, and will dig, chase and jump until he drops.

Schapendoes

He may be an easy-going dog, but his
hair is anything but that: he needs daily
grooming. Being affectionate and warm, he
rather enjoys the bonding experience. High
maintenance, he is also a high jumper, and
as a much rarer relative of the collie he is
exceptionally agile and active.

Cocker Spaniel

Never too far away, this Spaniel wants nothing more than to be your best friend. Determined, placid and playful, he loves dashing around in the snow — but it won't be long before he's running back to check up on you.

Shiba Inu

This little Japanese dog is spirited, agile and quick-footed. Most impressive in mountainous terrain, the snow is no challenge for him — he actually quite likes it.

Belgian Griffon

Being very small and almost entirely made up of beard, this toy dog would struggle in the snow without his snowsuit. Loving, devoted and full of self-importance, he doesn't mind being dressed up so long as it's for his own good and makes his owner happy.

Springer Spaniel

Springy by name, springy by nature; this dog takes a brief lie down in the snow to cool off before leaping back into action. Carefree and dutiful, he'll do any job you ask him to and he'll love every second.

Springer Spaniel and Golden Retriever

These two make a playful pair, and judging by all the footprints they have been at it for a while!

West Highland Terrier

Looking a bit lost without something or someone to play with, he is a bossy and authoritative character who's not afraid to tell you what he wants. A devoted and loyal dog, he is also strong-minded; he'll wait for you to catch up only to run off on his own again.

Cockapoo

He is sociable, affectionate and perpetually cheerful.
The snow can't dampen his spirits; he's just happy to be
wherever you are. Not the hardiest of dogs, what he lacks
in muscle he makes up for in enthusiasm — this curly
chap will play until his paws freeze.

Samoyeds

Known for their constant 'smile', these happy dogs are most at home in the snow. Maintaining puppy-like playfulness into adulthood, age is nothing but a number for these playmates. It does mean they need to be kept occupied, or their excitement can turn into chewing and barking.

Weimaraner

He may look a little wrinkly just now, but this big-eared pup will soon grow into his skin to become a muscular athlete. No walk is too long, no fence is too high, no snow is too deep. A lover of all things outdoors, he can be wilful and restless without proper training.

Airedale Terrier

Whilst hanging out of the car window is most dog's dream, this curious scamp can't wait to just get out into the snow. Always ready to cause some mischief, he is an adventurer and comedian. Outdoor activity is a necessity for him and a relief for his owners.

Labrador and Dachshund

The dachshund may have shorter legs, but he's determined, quick on his feet and unfazed by his playmate's size advantage. His flat paws also stop him sinking into the snow. Whilst he can be tentative and grumpy, he has been brought out of his shell by his leggy friend's trademark oafish playfulness.

Irish Wolfhound

This giant dog is surprisingly graceful and placid despite his intimidating size. Bred for hunting by sight, he has exceptionally keen vision — even against a snowy backdrop — and is always ready to run after anything that moves.

Golden Retriever

Never one to frown, he's a stable, jolly dog who loves being part of the family. You can tell by his grin that he's not suffering from the winter blues.

Schnoodle

This Schnauzer-Poodle cross is an unpredictable and charming character. Intelligent and obedient, he is easy to train. His winter coat, however, is less easily tameable, and with his love of adventure and the great outdoors you can expect a lot of trips to the groomer.

Sheltie

Despite her carefree appearance, this herding dog
is one of the smartest canine's out there. She's
immensely trainable and obedient, as well as
being athletic and agile. Perfect indoors or out,
she loves both work and play.

Jack Russell

A lover of burrowing, this little guy will tear up your garden and then pretend he didn't do it. Thankfully, the snow is more forgiving than your flowerbeds. He's intelligent and energetic, so it's best to keep him occupied on long walks — then he'd rather snuggle up on your sofa than chew it.

Crossbreed

Little legs aren't always a disadvantage for a
snow-lover, as this determined dog is proving.

Golden Retriever

This festive Retriever takes a moment to enjoy the snow.

Labrador

He loves to get involved, but this chocolate Lab might have been a little too enthusiastic about the snow and now he's got to put up with a cold nose. He's a hardy dog and used to the cold weather though, so he doesn't mind too much.

Belgian Malinois

One of the most energetic dogs of them all, getting this Malinois to stand still for a photo can be tricky. Bounding in and out of the snow, he'll be gone before the next flurry settles. Filled with energy, this live wire can be a handful, but he is easily trained and loves a new challenge.

Staffordshire Bull Terriers

Bred as fighting dogs, this pair has an aggressive side. But these muscular playmates are known to be fun loving and nurturing, and are soppy lapdogs when it comes to their owners. They may play rough, but playing in the snow lets off some of their boundless energy and helps keep these two cool-headed.

British Bulldog and Central Asian Shepherd Dog

The winter blues are clearly not affecting these two as they play rough and tumble.

Miniature Labradoodle and Labradoodle

With his calm and amiable nature, this Labradoodle is a dog to look up to – and his miniature friend certainly does! An intelligent and physical pair, the snow is just an added bonus on their daily walk.

Border Collie

High-energy, high-intelligence, high-maintenance: this dog needs a lot of exercise and mental stimulation to reach his full potential. He's ready and raring to go all year round, so forget about the snow and throw that ball!

Border Collies

Enjoying the snow with their paws around each other, these two are the best of pals.

English Cocker Spaniel

Alert and resilient, this little Spaniel won't allow herself to be fazed by the snow! Ever the optimist, she thinks she is bigger than she is, and happily charges around for hours before collapsing on her beloved owner's lap for some much-needed affection.

Breed Unknown

This contemplative dog might be taking a moment to take in the snowy landscape, but he'll soon be ready to gallop across it.

Border Collie

A show off at times, this clever Collie parades his unusual sable colouring in the snow. A capable worker, he is also a natural showman and enjoys performing tricks and showing off his agility. But don't let him get too confident or he'll run rings around you.

Labradors

Easy going and non-competitive, these Labradors get along just fine with one another. Dutifully awaiting their next order, this loyal gang will forget all about the snow until they've completed their owner's every command.

Miniature Dachshund

This 'sausage dog' may not be ideally built for deep snow, but he's rugged and outgoing so it doesn't stop him charging around. He's a friendly dog, but is independent minded and loves the sound of his own voice, so can make a great — and compact — watchdog.

Miniature American Eskimo Dog

Inquisitive and animated, he is an investigator and loves to know everyone's business. He's a quick learner because he's eager to please, and is one of the most obedient and trainable dogs out there. He is, however, quick to get bored, but he'll play in the snow for hours – it's his favourite thing.

Siberian Huskies

Confident pack animals, this team is efficient, hard-working and enduring. Bred for their speed and resilience, they are the sprinters of the sled dog world and will pull a sled across kilometres of snowy terrain with ease.

Labrador-greyhound

There is nothing this dog loves more than feeling the wind in his ears and the snow under his paws.

Dogue de Bordeaux

In a moment of calm, these French Mastiffs take in their snowy surroundings before charging off again.

137

Old English Sheepdog

These floppy-haired dogs are expert herders, and can move quickly despite their shaggy appearance. Wearing their permanent coat, they are most at home when they are outdoors. The clownish pair maintain a puppy-like enthusiasm for life, but often need to be taught a few lessons by a firm owner.

CROSSBREED

It's been a long day of playing and this tired pooch is just about ready for a nap, but there's no need to go all the way back to his bed when he has a thick coat and a fresh blanket of snow.